WE ARE ALL CONNECTE[...]

ARE YOU OPEN AND RECEPTIVE TO
ABSORBING KNOWLEDGE FROM THOSE
AROUND YOU?

OBSERVE: GAIN FROM ANOTHER'S
EXPERIENCE. WE ALL HAVE
SOMETHING UNIQUE TO SHARE.
ENGAGE THE WORLD WITH
COMPASSION, PATIENCE AND
GENEROSITY.

Library of Congress-in Publication-Data
Bardo, Rosalie
Calm Your Heart/ by Rosalie Bardo;
Interior Design by Rosalie Bardo
Summary: Mindfulness Journal with
meditative art, affirmations
and 26 writing prompts
to assist in reframing your day.
ISBN: 978-0-9978738-5-6
Library of Congress Control Number
available upon request

Printed in the United States of America
Distributed by: GreyHouse Press
Cover and book design by Rosalie Bardo
Cover font: Playlist Script
Interior font: Playlist Script
Glacial Indifference

MINDFULNESS JOURNAL

Walk in love

DESCRIBE THE SIGNIFICANT SHIFTS IN
YOUR LIFE OVER THE PAST 3 YEARS

have your interests changed + career + relationships + family

_____

_____

_____

_____

_____

_____

_____

_____

_____

_____

_____

ARE YOUR CURRENT ENERGIES FLOWING IN
THE DIRECTION YOU ASPIRE TO GO?

_____

_____

THE WORRY IN YOUR HEART + THE ANGER + THE PAIN

share your struggle with me...

_____

_____

_____

_____

_____

_____

_____

_____

_____

_____

_____

_____

_____

_____

_____

YOU ARE WORTHY OF ALL GOOD THINGS

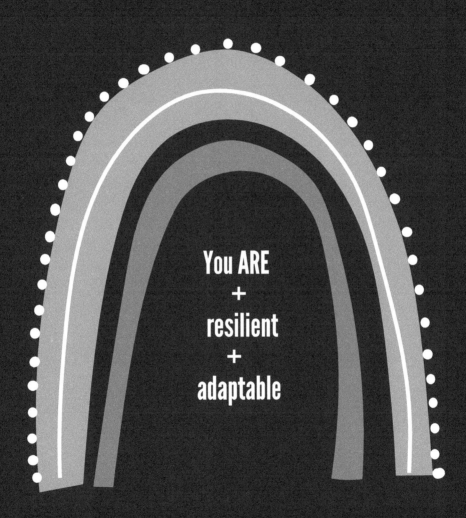

DO YOU RESPOND TO OTHERS OR REACT?

it helps to pause before speaking...

_____

_____

_____

_____

_____

_____

_____

_____

_____

_____

WHAT TRIGGERS YOU?
BE HONEST

_____

_____

_____

_____

THIS IS YOUR

SACRED JOURNEY

WHO INSPIRES YOU?

tell me about their admirable traits...

_____

_____

_____

_____

_____

_____

_____

_____

_____

DO YOU CARE ABOUT ENCOURAGING OTHERS?
WHY + WHY NOT?

_____

_____

_____

_____

DO YOU ALLOW FEAR
TO DICTATE YOUR CHOICES?

BE BRAVE. BE BOLD.
TRUST IN YOUR ABILITIES.

DO YOU BELIEVE IN THE POWER OF
SPEAKING DAILY AFFIRMATIONS?

begin a list, I'll start...

1. I AM KIND TO MYSELF AND OTHERS.

KEEP GOING.
READ YOUR LIST ALOUD

WHAT WOULD YOU CHANGE ABOUT OUR WORLD?

share your hope with me...

_____

_____

_____

_____

_____

_____

_____

_____

_____

_____

_____

_____

_____

_____

_____

ARE YOU WALKING THROUGH LIFE WITH GUILT?

shame can be all consuming, share with me your story...

_____

_____

_____

_____

_____

_____

_____

_____

_____

_____

_____

_____

_____

_____

_____

_____

YOU ARE FREE FROM THE JUDGEMENT AND CONTROL OF OTHERS

ARE YOU HAPPY FOR OTHERS OR ENVIOUS?

tell me about it...

A GENTLE REMINDER TO APPRECIATE
ALL THAT YOU HAVE

HOW DO YOU FEEL TODAY?

are you experiencing joy + depression + anxiety?

share your day with me...

_____

_____

_____

_____

_____

_____

_____

_____

_____

_____

_____

WHAT WOULD YOU CHANGE
ABOUT YOUR ROUTINE?

_____

_____

_____

_____

_____

EMPATHY VS. EGO

BALANCED

BREATHE IN

RELEASE THE
FRUSTRATION

WHAT ARE YOU GRIEVING?

a person + place + an unspoken dream + a hidden desire

_____

_____

_____

_____

_____

_____

_____

_____

_____

_____

_____

_____

_____

_____

_____

_____

_____

DO YOU ACKNOWLEDGE YOUR GRIEF OR TRY TO SUFFOCATE IT?

_____

WHAT ARE THE SIMPLE YET BEAUTIFUL THINGS SURROUNDING YOU?

LOOK AROUND.
DESCRIBE THEM.

WHO WAS THE LAST PERSON YOU INTERACTED WITH?

how did they make you feel? Energized or drained?

_____

_____

_____

_____

_____

_____

_____

_____

_____

_____

_____

ARE YOU ABLE TO SHOW UP AS YOUR TRUE SELF AROUND THOSE YOU LOVE?

_____

_____

you are limitless

WHEN WAS YOUR LAST SOCIAL MEDIA BREAK?
Take this journal outside + Turn off the TV + Put down the phone

_____

_____

_____

_____

_____

_____

_____

_____

HOW DOES THE FRESH AIR FEEL?

_____

_____

_____

_____

_____

_____

WHY DO YOU USE SOCIAL NETWORKING APPS?
IF YOU DON'T, TELL ME WHY.

WHERE WOULD YOU TRAVEL IF YOU COULD GO ANYWHERE?

Bound by nothing

REFLECT ON THE HELPERS IN YOUR LIFE

Who shows up for you + who is always there?

WHAT BRINGS YOU PEACE?

a person + place + hobby + ritual

Your favorite book + movie + song

SHARE IT WITH ME...

_____

_____

_____

_____

_____

_____

_____

_____

_____

_____

_____

_____

_____

AFFIRMATIONS TO PONDER

I am capable

I don't need validation from others

I am forgiving

I am living without judgement

I am worthy of all good things

I am mentally and physically healthy

I am grateful for this journey

I am abundant in every aspect of my life

sit with the idea
that your life
won't stay the same

+

change is constant

WHY ARE YOU ANGRY?

if you aren't mad in this moment, what infuriates you?

_____

_____

_____

_____

_____

_____

_____

_____

_____

_____

_____

_____

_____

_____

_____

HAVE YOU EXPLORED THE ORIGIN OF THIS UNIVERSAL EMOTION?

CLOSE YOUR EYES.
TAKE 10
DEEP BREATHS.

REPEAT.

DO YOU CONFORM TO
SOCIETAL NORMS?

HAVE YOU EXAMINED THIS SUBTLE SOCIAL PRESSURE?

ARE YOU CHOOSING AUTHENTICITY?

WHO ARE YOUR FRIENDS?

reflect on the common thread that connects you

_____

_____

_____

_____

_____

_____

_____

_____

_____

_____

_____

_____

_____

_____

_____

HOW OFTEN DO YOU LAUGH?

RELIGIOUS + SPIRITUAL + AGNOSTIC?

is the quality of your daily life impacted by your beliefs?

SHARE WITH ME YOUR DAILY PRACTICES, ARE THEY ROOTED IN LOVE?

Exude Gratitude

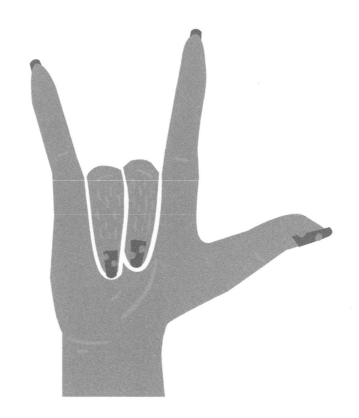

YOU. ARE. LOVED.

RECOUNT AN EVENT THAT BECAME A
TURNING POINT FOR YOU IN ADULTHOOD
achievement + accident + encounter + trauma

MET·A·MOR·PHO·SIS

A CHANGE OF THE FORM OR NATURE
OF A THING OR PERSON INTO A
COMPLETELY DIFFERENT ONE

CREATIVITY

RESIST

EXPLORE

WARRIOR

SIMPLIFY

ENERGY

receiving

ATTRACT ABUNDANCE

CALMNESS

WORDS HOLD POWER

GODDESS

AWARE

EXPANSION

DIVINE

fearless

MOVEMENT

PEACE

WALK IN LOVE

SPEAK INTO EXISTENCE

SACRED

i am

eternal

CONNECTION

EGO

WHIMSICAL

EMPOWERED

transparent

TRUTH

PURE

SELCOUTH

RESONATE

MEDITATION

bliss

CLARITY

PROTECTION

EMPATHY

INVITE

THANK YOU

compassion

READY

BECOMING

YES

TRANSFORMATION

HEALING

VAST

QUESTION

MANIFEST

illusion

ILLUMINATE

purify

TRUST

WRITE

elated

ADAPT

SUSTAINABLE

YOU. ARE. LOVED.

CPSIA information can be obtained
at www.ICGtesting.com
Printed in the USA
LVHW071622270521
688666LV00039B/1627